You need to hear this
shit

and here you are living

despite it all.

- Rupi Kaur

Arkopaul

ISBN 9798414775508

Arkopaul

You need to hear this shit.

Arkopaul Das

Arkopaul

OTHER BOOKS BY ARKOPAUL DAS:

THE DEAD VETERAN

INSOMNIAC

LIMOUSINE

LIVE ON THE EDGE

SOCIOPATH: DECEITFUL GAME

Arkopaul

You need to hear this shit

Arkopaul

You need to hear this shit

Arkopaul

Dedicated to myself cos I probably need to hear this shit a lot more than anyone else.

Arkopaul

The ultimate truth to life is being happy. If you are not happy, nothing, absolutely nothing is worth it. Your happiness comes first before anyone else's. You don't have to be a selfish bitch; you can be kind and grateful to people who deserve it, but if you see someone or something is tampering with your peace of mind; your happiness, it's not worth it. Because if you are not happy, nothing is worth it.

Arkopaul

Money doesn't bring you happiness, but it takes away all the things that make you unhappy. It won't fix everything. Like if you lose a loved one or go through a bad breakup, no amount of money will fix it. If you have money at least you aren't worried about paying your bills, or getting food, or travelling, or whatever doing you like. It's better to be rich and sad than broke and sad.

Arkopaul

Nothing is worth losing your self-respect. We often put ourselves in weird positions and let other people treat us like shit, especially when we are in love or when we don't wanna lose friends. We give them chances after chances, and we tolerate whatever they do just because we don't wanna lose them. But ask yourself, do you really wanna be with someone who costs you your self-respect? No. Get the fuck out of there.

Arkopaul

You are your best friend so treat yourself like one. You know yourself the best, you have literally been with yourself throughout the darkest periods of your life when there was no one around. Not your close friends, not your partner, not your family. All the mental battles you have fought, cooped up in your room alone, it was just you. And you survived 100% of those days. You are the best friend you wish you had, so treat yourself right.

Arkopaul

Everyone is temporary. At least most people, except maybe for your parents or your family or someone. Someday someone will come into your life and will stay forever but you don't know who that is or when they will come into your life. Until then, just know that people will come and go. It's okay if someone broke up with you, or if you lose touch with someone, or if you stop talking to someone and get distant. It's okay. Neither of you lost each other; it's just life taking its natural course.

Arkopaul

You are alone. I won't bullshit you or try to console you. You come into this world alone and you leave it alone. It doesn't matter if there is a room filled with people on your deathbed, it's still just you dying. So, stop expecting people to constantly tag along with you, support you, or help you. If someone does, great, if they don't, great, you do you. So, it's okay if you have no one to talk to or if you have to sit alone in your college, or if you are just an introvert who doesn't vibe with anyone. It sucks to be alone but you have to accept the reality for what it is. Stay strong and work your way through life.

Arkopaul

Expectation isn't a bad thing. Expectation is a standard you set for yourself, and if you someone fails to meet it, just slowly cut them off.

People do not owe you shit. The world does not owe you anything. Everyone is busy handling their own problems, too busy to care for yours. It's only the closest people, like your parents or your best friends would be the only ones who'd care for you but even then, they might not. People will disappoint you, and it's okay as long as they are not being toxic or hurting you in some way.

Arkopaul

Things will never go the way you imagined. You will go through pain, trauma, heartbreaks, and also good things like success and happiness. All of it is normal.

Arkopaul

No one is too busy to make time for you. If they genuinely care for you, they will reach out to you and talk to you. They will answer your texts and calls, and will ask you about your day. They won't let you go to bed wondering if you are enough.

Arkopaul

If you explain your hurt and still get hurt, stop talking. Turn around, and no matter how much it breaks you apart, leave. They won't change, they never do.

Arkopaul

This one is especially for introverts and people who are insecure. When you walk into a room full of people, focus on what you think about them instead of what they think about you. Remember everyone has their secrets and insecurities no matter how put together they might seem on the outside.

Arkopaul

Whenever something traumatic happens, allow yourself to grief. Grief felicitates the healing process. You cannot skip it and pretend everything is okay. Sit down, take a breath, cry if you need to and that's how you get through it. It doesn't make you weak, it's okay.

Arkopaul

If something makes you happy, something that doesn't harm anyone or endanger your future, just do it. If you want to get that tattoo, get it, you wanna travel to that place, go for it, you wanna confess your feelings to someone, do it, you feel like having ice cream at 2 in the morning, fucking do it.

If something makes you happy, it doesn't have to make sense to others.

Arkopaul

If you aren't happy with what you already have, you won't ever be happy with what you will have. Happiness comes from within; it can't be derived from materials and money alone. If you are not at peace with the person you are, no amount of money will make you feel better. You will keep chasing and chasing until you are burnt out.

Arkopaul

You probably have heard this one before, but let go of things that are not in your control. The only thing you can control is yourself; sometimes you can't even control yourself. You can't control how people will act and react, you can only control how you feel about it. You can't control life either. It will take you where it wants to, either way, so just sit back, relax, and let it.

Arkopaul

Make friends who add value to your life, or else just don't. Don't force yourself to be friends with people who don't respect or understand you, in fact, brings you down consistently. There is no point tagging along with these people. You will meet people who will love you, support you, help you grow and they are the ones you are gonna wanna keep in your life.

Arkopaul

In the age of heartbreaks and depression, stay close to anybody that makes you feel alive.

Arkopaul

Failure is important. And it is okay. You will repeatedly fail, just keep at it. But also know when to bail out instead of obsessing over something or someone that clearly isn't working out for you because there are probably so many better opportunities and people you are ignoring while being obsessed over this one thing.

Arkopaul

It's okay if you feel like dropping out of your college. Loads of people do it these days. Often people with a million degrees still get stuck at dead end jobs with no momentum. But before you jump the gun, make a detailed list of pros and cons of dropping out and also what you want to do instead. If you want to freelance, or have a business/start up idea make a detailed plan of how you will pursue it and how it might turn out. Be very sure of it basically and then go for it. In India, opportunities are already scarce and competition is insane, so make sure you are up for the grind especially when you don't have a piece of paper backing you up.

Arkopaul

Be kind to everyone who deserves it but don't take shit from any motherfucker. Show them their place and their worth and go slay.

Arkopaul

Always be straightforward. I know a lot of people who are petty and don't speak up and bottle up everything inside, but I earnestly urge you to be real and speak up about whatever is bothering you. You are doing yourself a favour. And if your significant other doesn't get it or care, stop begging that person to understand and leave.

Arkopaul

People go to therapy to deal with issues that people who should go to therapy, cause.

Arkopaul

Once you heal your heart and get over them you will realize they are not special. They never were. It was the love you had for them that made them special. Once that love is gone, once you stop looking at them the way you did before you will understand how ordinary they really were.

Arkopaul

If you are looking out for yourself, taking care of yourself, protecting yourself, then you are not being selfish. If someone tries to gaslight you into believing that you are being selfish just because you are trying to do what's right for you, then fuck them, you don't need that negativity.

Arkopaul

A lot of people fake their depression to get clout online and I am aware of that but you don't know who is faking it and who is going through it for real. So don't try to bully anyone or try to call them out, just be nice to them regardless.

Arkopaul

Do not promise random things especially when you are in a good mood. Some people might actually take it seriously and feel bad when you fail to live up to it while others might try to use the said promise to their advantage and make you feel bad instead.

Thank them for leaving you because you probably wouldn't have been able to walk away from them no matter how much they hurt you.

Arkopaul

Let your mind wonder, dream, fantasize and live in a utopian reality if you want. It is fine, but also get out of that phase and move along with your real life instead of drowning in it. You might feel super aesthetic until all the bills that are due and the deadlines that you are supposed to meet hits you.

Arkopaul

People never show their true colours when you first meet them or when you first start dating them. Remember, that the person you believe to be your whole world might turn out to be someone you could have never imagined.

Arkopaul

Similarly, don't overjudge people who show their true colours from day 1 and actually leaves a bad impression on you. These people are at least wearing their heart on their sleeves and being real about who they are instead of switching personalities.

Do not encourage inconsistency. These people are dealing with their own conflicts and aren't sure of their own lives so they will push and pull constantly changing their attitudes and behaviours and treating you accordingly. This is straight toxic and you don't wanna get tangled up in their mess.

Arkopaul

If you are not sure of yourself or going through something of your own then don't pursue a relationship expecting someone else to fix you when you can barely fix yourself. Don't lead them on. Relationship is a big commitment and requires a lot of effort and determination. If you are looking for something casual, then make it very obvious from the start cos the other person could be looking for something serious and might get hurt when they find out that you are not down for it.

Stop using your childhood trauma as an excuse to be an asshole.

Arkopaul

Sometimes you have to heal from the things you didn't deserve and it's okay.

Arkopaul

If someone feels like they won to take some sort of moral high ground and feel better about themselves, let them. It doesn't affect you or your life in any way. It doesn't matter if they won some sort of mental battle, you were not in competition with them, you have your own life to handle so let them have their win and you do you.

Arkopaul

At some point you might have to stop talking to the person you thought you would marry and that's life.

Arkopaul

Life has no meaning. That's why you can do whatever you want with it, or even end it. Treat it like an empty canvas waiting to be filled with colours.

Arkopaul

Accept and embrace your flaws and no one can use them against you. Be vocal about them, be sure about them, don't let them bog you down. Everyone has their flaws and embarrassing moments, it's not just you.

Arkopaul

This one is for parents. Stop projecting your failed dreams and fantasies on your children, let them decide what they want to do in life and support and guide them. That's all they need.

Arkopaul

Always be vocal about what you feel except for the places where you know what you feel does not matter.

Arkopaul

Nothing is inherently embarrassing.

Arkopaul

If they make you feel bad about expressing how you felt, then they are simply gaslighting you. You shouldn't have to apologise for feeling bad for something or something that you are going through. This is a toxic trait and you don't need these people in your life.

Stop running after revenge. People will tell you that success is the best revenge, but it's not. Not caring about their existence and just living your life, successfully or otherwise, is the best revenge. Remember, if you wanna be successful, you should do it for yourself and your family, you shouldn't do it because you feel like you have something to prove to someone because there's a good chance that even after working hard as fuck you might fall short of that success and feel unsatisfied and unfulfilled because you couldn't take revenge on these people. Never fall into that rabbit hole.

Arkopaul

Theodore Roosevelt once said "Believe you can and you are already halfway there". I couldn't agree more but also believe in something that is realistic and achievable. If you believe you are going to be the next Elon Musk, you are not gonna be halfway there.

It's better to die with memories than to die with dreams.

Arkopaul

If you are in your 20s and feel lost just know that it's fine. You are supposed to be lost, explore, experience new things, find what your love and passion, have your fair share or heartbreaks and failures. You are not supposed to have it all figured out just yet so just take it easy, will you?

Arkopaul

Nothing scares me more than "Turn on your camera and unmute yourself".

Arkopaul

Stop chasing simulations. Your social media or the people you hang out with or the stuff that you do. It's okay to feel bored. You don't need constant sensory overload because you will become dependent on them and won't be able to function once these simulations are gone.

Learning to accept things that you can't do shit about is immensely powerful. However, that does not mean that you should skip the other stages of grief when something terrible happens.

Arkopaul

People will tell you that respect matters and you should seek respect instead of attention. I disagree. The only person you need to seek respect from is yourself. You should respect the fuck out of yourself. If other people respect you, that's great, if they don't, that's great. Be a good person and don't go out looking for respect, or attention.

Arkopaul

Stop telling people "There are other people out there who have it much worse than you." Pain and depression can't be compared. What you are doing is being a dick and invalidating their feels, telling them they are not allowed to feel the way they do because other people apparently have it worse. This does not make anyone feel better it will only make them feel worse.

Arkopaul

Stop romanticizing mental illness. We do need to talk about it but don't make it seem like it's nothing, it's just a normal thing that everyone goes through. It's not that light and casual. There are so many people with depression who probably lost the battle and gave up on their life as you are reading this right now. It is not a joke, get help, reach out.

Arkopaul

Try to relax and have a little more fun in your life. Stop taking life too seriously especially when obsessing over life is not working out at all. Let it flow and vibe along to it cos at the end of the day if you are not having fun, it's not worth it.

Arkopaul

Tough situations don't always make tough people.

Sometimes you just end up broken and traumatized, period.

Arkopaul

If someone is playing hard to get, stop chasing.

Arkopaul

You can't be a good person throughout your whole life because if that is what you aspire to be - just purely good, then the world will take advantage of your kindness and make you crash and burn. So, you know what, sometimes you gotta break some hearts and kick some asses.

Arkopaul

The world doesn't owe you shit. It will be unforgiving and cruel and in fact try to fuck you up as much as it can. Never expect the world to empathize, sympathize or understand and care about how you feel. No one gives a shit.

Arkopaul

Some people will tell you that this isn't true, because you owe the world some kindness, gratefulness and gratitude but well that's a utopian dream and little else. If the world worked that way, then it wouldn't be as fucked up as it is. Look around, there's only a handful of genuine people left out there where everyone is tryna exploit everyone else.

Arkopaul

You have heard this one before but I will say it again. Time doesn't heal your wounds; it simply forces you to live with it.

Arkopaul

When we break up, we are heartbroken not only because the love of our life left us but because deep inside, we believe that we will never experience this love or this level of connection with anyone ever again.

Arkopaul

Life is a lot different based on how you choose to look at it because I swear there's a lot of people out there in a much better position than you, earning a lot, got the love of their life by their side, got anything they want but yet they are constantly miserable just because they choose to look at life in a particular way instead of counting their blessings.

Arkopaul

Money might not buy me happiness but I would rather be rich and sad than broke and sad anyway.

Arkopaul

Stop arguing with people especially about random shit that simply doesn't matter or will affect your life in any way. They want to win the conversation and it's absolutely fine, let them, what do you have to prove?

Arkopaul

You will fail in life repeatedly. Over and over again. And that's completely fine. Either get back up and try it again or try something different instead of obsessing over something you are clearly not good at. At the end of the day, try to enjoy whatever you are doing because see, you will fail in life even after doing something you don't enjoy so you might as well fail doing something you love.

Arkopaul

Most of the things and people in your life is temporary if not all. Including situations. Sometimes it will get better, sometimes it will be shit and you will suffer, but it won't be the same. I won't be one of those people who tells you that it gets better cos in my experience it doesn't. It only gets worse and well, that's fine, that's the life you are awarded with.

Arkopaul

Stop running after huge goals and then getting hurt when you fail to accomplish them. Sometimes even getting out of bed and taking a shower is hard as fuck. So calm down, set small goals, do the best you can every day and vibe along.

You are never too old to start something new.

Arkopaul

If you start missing them, just remember they don't deserve a badass mf like you.

Arkopaul

How they treat you when you are not on good terms with them says a lot about them. Love and respect do not fade away just because you had a fight.

Arkopaul

Sometimes people know exactly what they are doing and still continue doing it. They will repeatedly apologise and do the same shit over and over again because sorry means nothing to them and holds on value.

Arkopaul

Let people do what they want, their actions will determine how much they value the relationship. At the end of the day, you cannot control him or her, they will do what they want regardless of your possessiveness. So, trust them, and if they break your trust repeatedly, well that's it then, right?

Arkopaul

Healing can be an incredibly weird phase. One day you will feel super motivated ready to take on the world and move on with your life and the next day you will wake crying from the ache in your heart and think the world has ended for you.

I cannot stress this enough but self-love is so important. I have said this before and I will reiterate it again, love yourself fully and deeply and never let anyone challenge your self-respect and dignity. You will never find someone like you ever again in your life.

Arkopaul

Alone time is important. You don't have to constantly communicate or surround yourself with random people. It's okay to be alone once in a while and bath in some peace and solitude. Take a break and reflect on your thoughts and learn to live and be comfortable with yourself, in your own skin. Once you are comfortable with yourself and don't need any external influences anymore to go on with your life you will become immensely powerful.

Even at your absolute best, you will never be right for the wrong person.

If you have to beg for it, you already lost it.

Arkopaul

Confidence is important. Most people will look at you the way you look at yourself.

Arkopaul

Education and degrees are important especially in a country like India where paper talks more than practical skills and work experience talks more than determination and dedication, however, it's not worth it if it's costing you your mental health. You only have one life, make sure you are doing what you really want to do.

Arkopaul

Stop working extra hard. Hard work alone won't guarantee you success. Luck is an important factor that successful people don't wanna talk about because it makes them look weak but if you study their lives carefully you will notice that in most situations, they simply got lucky. Others might not have caught the break that they did even after working harder than them. What you need to do is be smart about your decisions so that you don't have to work extra hard and exhaust yourself.

Arkopaul

No one can fix you except for yourself. People can be there for you, support you, motivate you, but at the end of the day it's just you vs you. Only you can fix yourself.

We all work in our own timelines. Stop comparing your life with people who are seemingly doing better in life and going forward while you are stuck and lost. They don't know your life; they haven't lived your life. Keep your head straight and do the best you can.

Arkopaul

You can't win unless your mind is stronger than your emotions. If your emotions and your heart get the better of you then you will lose every time. It's not easy to master this technique but if you can keep a rational mind under strenuous circumstances then you have already won.

Your past doesn't define who you are. It may have been great or absolutely traumatic but it does not mean that your future will be the same. Stop living in the past.

Arkopaul

You owe it to yourself to be consistent, you owe it to yourself to be disciplined, you owe it to yourself focused.

Arkopaul

Growth is choosing happiness over history. Growth is leaving the past behind and moving forward.

Arkopaul

Be open to new opportunities. Sometimes we have a goal in life and we become obsessed and confine ourselves in it and become blind to other possible opportunities. If you are failing at your current goal repeatedly and getting burnt out trying over and over again, it's okay to take a step back and explore something new. Who knows, maybe you will discover a new passion or new side of yourself and create a new goal in your mind.

Arkopaul

Everyone is going through something but you can't help everyone. That's the harsh truth. Stop being so hard on yourself.

Arkopaul

Please don't call them selfish when someone is on the verge of killing themselves. Suicide is not selfish; suicide is not about passing the pain onto someone else. Stop making it all about you. Suicide is about that person dealing with his own demons hoping to end it all and rid the world of himself to make it a better place. It is not selfish; on the contrary it is one of the most self-less act in the whole motherfucking world.

Arkopaul

Expectations from your close friends and family is not a bad thing. It is a standard you are setting for yourself, and if someone can't match that and give you the bare minimum then it's not worth investing in them.

Arkopaul

We don't just miss people, we miss the moments, the memories, the life we could have had with them.

Arkopaul

You don't live once; you live every day. You die once.

Unless you love someone, who doesn't love you back.

Then you die every day.

Arkopaul

You are not supposed to stay the same. You are not supposed to be the same person that you were 5 years ago. You are constantly growing, changing, evolving, your personality, life style, thoughts, opinions, philosophies, intellect, fashion, everything is constantly changing and there is nothing wrong with it as long as you continue to learn and be better.

Arkopaul

Be so strong that you can wish for someone else's happiness while you are breaking down crying on your cold bathroom floor at 3 in the morning.

Arkopaul

Instead of being afraid of losing people, be afraid of losing yourself when you are with them.

Arkopaul

You will never be too much for someone who can't get enough of you.

Arkopaul

A wise man once said "If you are overthinking about all the worst possible scenarios that could happen, then you are making yourself going through the same shit twice."

Arkopaul

Whenever the memories hit you that one night and you feel like stalking them or calling them or going back, just never forget the disrespect. Never forget the fact that you gave them your everything and got fuckall back. Remember why it ended in the first place, remember the hurt, the pain, the fights, the anger, emotions, frustrations, the lack of respect. Remember it all but never go back.

Arkopaul

Let go of what let go of you.

Arkopaul

If they miss you and try to reach out, don't go back. Let them miss you, let them realize that they had you and couldn't treat you right.

Arkopaul

You make them feel special and give them a sense of belonging not because you solely understand them but you see all their flaws and imperfections and still choose to love them deeply.

Someday you will hear a love song or watch a romantic movie and no one will come to your mind.

Arkopaul

I love all things aesthetic. From poetries, to a walk in the park, to sunsets, to the moon and the stars, to having take-out while we watch a comic book movie, to deciphering random pieces of abstract art and listening to that one song that no one has even heard off and exploring unknown territories alone, I love all things aesthetic.

Arkopaul

Always remember that overthinking makes us suffer more in imagination than in reality. 90% of the things we are anxious about never even happens in real life. We just assume that it will and beat ourselves up over it.

Arkopaul

It doesn't matter how you look, not your coarse skin, or the colour of it, or the way your face looks or the way your nose bends or the way your hair flows or the way your lips open when you talk. It doesn't matter how you look, if you are a nice person, you are beautiful and don't let nobody tell you otherwise.

Arkopaul

There is nothing prettier than a city at 5 in the morning. With its melancholic deserted streets and cold winds.

Arkopaul

Stop watering dead plants.

Arkopaul

People tell us to be honest, we grow up hearing that honesty is the best policy. But know when to lie. It is not always possible to be 100% honest and real, you gotta put on a front sometimes. Lie when it is necessary, when it helps you in some way, it is fine. The only person you need to be honest with is yourself. Never lie or bullshit yourself.

Arkopaul

If I said it once, I've said it a hundred million times. Depression is real.

It sucks when you are sitting in the middle of a room filled with people and yet you are so fucking lonely and broken.

Arkopaul

If you see anyone going through depression, assure them that you are there for them. Urge them to speak out, but don't force. Urge them to seek professional help and give them a shoulder to cry on. There are so many people suffering from depression and other mental illnesses in this country and yet it is a taboo, and yet no one speaks about it. It's about time we normalize it and not romanticize it. It's about time we make each other feel less alone and stop them from the point of no return. We need help and we only have each other for it.

Arkopaul

When you go through something terrible like a break up, instead of resorting to self-destructive behaviours like getting drunk and high, you need to find what you are passionate about. You need to find a hobby. You also need to know that it is okay and completely normal to feel like shit. You need to know that with time, it will be okay. I know you don't wanna hear this, but I will keep it real with you, it will be okay.

Arkopaul

Learn to help other people without any ulterior motives or intentions. Help them because that's what you do. Don't ask for anything in return expect for basic respect.

Try to make the best out of yourself because the other options are either you can wallow in misery and compare yourself with others, or you can kill yourself. And I definitely don't recommend either, but then again, I understand sometimes we just don't have a choice.

Arkopaul

There is no karma. Stop waiting for them to get punished for their sins. You are indirectly holding on to them and destroying yourself. It's not worth it. They will live a perfectly happy life even after killing you and you will kill yourself further when you constantly expect them to face some sort of punishment but all you see is how happy they are without you. Let go of it and move on.

It's okay to talk to yourself when you don't have anyone around you. It doesn't mean you are crazy. It is a liberating feeling and it makes us feel less alone. After all we are all that we have so why not talk to our own selves right, someone who genuinely understands us?

Arkopaul

People who make you smile on your bad days are precious.

If you are overthinking about something in particular, remember we are on a rock floating around a burning ball of gas in the middle of endless cosmos. The universe does not care and nothing matters in the grand scheme of things. Take a breath.

Arkopaul

Happiness looks beautiful on you.

Arkopaul

Social media has become an important part of our lives. If someone talks about sad shit constantly, let them. For some people, social media is the only escape and it's okay. I know social media also makes us compare each other more and feel shit but that does not mean that suicide and mental health problems didn't exist before this, it is a whole different conversation altogether. My point is to use social media if it makes you feel better, rant as much as you want, it's okay.

Arkopaul

People never show their true colours at first. They all seem perfect and you will vibe along great, it's only much later when they show what they truly are. People break off their friendships and relationships after years and years. So never forget that people have the ability to change in the blink of an eye.

Arkopaul

Learn to live in the present. Don't ruin the moment thinking about your past or your future, two things that are not in your control. All you have is the present moment, the now. Make the "now" worth it at all cost because that's all you got.

Arkopaul

I hate seeing people self-harm or resort to self-destructive behaviours but you know what, I get it. I have been there myself, when you are pushed to the edge you tend to numb one pain with another.

Arkopaul

Stop going for rebounds. If you haven't healed you are just ignoring the pain and the agony buried in your heart, going out in the world and looking for some quick fix, but one day it will all come out hard and the person who fell for you will be ruined. Don't do this, rebounds always implode and blow up. Give yourself time to focus on other things until you are genuinely ready to give your heart again.

Arkopaul

Instead of focusing on all the things you don't have, focus on the things that you already have.

Arkopaul

Stop bullshitting yourself, if you feel like someone is not giving you that energy back, that attention, that respect you deserve, you are probably right. Have a serious conversation with your partner and clear things out instead of letting the misunderstanding build on.

Arkopaul

If you feel like giving up, remember the reason you held on for so long.

Your pain is not permanent. It is hypocritical of me to say this because I don't honestly believe it gets better, it only gets worse but still, I am here for some reason. I have been to the point of no return and I have still returned every time. I have lived through 100% of my worst days, I don't know how I did it but I did it. Earnest Hemingway once said "The sun also sets" but I would like to expand on it and say "The sun also sets, but it rises again every time."

Arkopaul

They knew exactly what they were doing to you, they just didn't give a fuck.

Arkopaul

Yes, you are stressed out and depressed and fucked up, but what you really need in life is coffee and a piercing.

Arkopaul

Everyone in your life will have a last day with you, and you don't know when that is so make every moment with them count.

Arkopaul

I don't need any more character development, I need to skip to that part of the story where I am successful and there's a crowd out there cheering me on.

Arkopaul

The people you lose when you are going through your healing phase are the ones who deserved to be with the unhealed version of you. Let them go.

Frugal living is underrated. See what you can get rid of in your house, pack them up, and keep them in one corner for a couple of weeks. If you didn't need to use these things over two weeks then get rid of them because you can probably live without these things forever.

Arkopaul

Nothing will be enough if you aren't already satisfied with what you have. You will keep asking for more and more and there's no end to that.

Arkopaul

Do you ever feel permanently exhausted? Like you haven't done shit all day and yet you are so mentally and physically drained out? Like getting out of the bed or going to your work is a pain? Like you can't tolerate people around you and just wanna be left alone?

Arkopaul

Whenever you feel like doing something, do it. Don't hold it off or give yourself any excuse. There is no right time to do it, in fact there's no time better than now.

Arkopaul

I don't look back and dwell in memories because love is too powerful a feeling to be bound by memories. I will either keep you in my heart always or I will cut you off completely.

Arkopaul

When nothing is going right for you, even after you are working your ass off to make ends meet, just let everything go for a second and breath in and out. Sometimes good things happen when you stop trying and forcing it.

Arkopaul

Happiness is the most luxurious and expensive thing to own in this decade.

Arkopaul

If you fight with me and win, you will lose.

Arkopaul

You are enough just the way you are. You are flawed, imperfect, your skin isn't smooth, your face doesn't have the conventional model ready looks, your life is not stable, your family is broken just like your heart, but the fact that you are still trying, still holding on, counts for something. This matters a lot. This makes you enough.

Arkopaul

Don't set aside your happiness now so that you can be happy in future. You don't know what the future holds for you. You don't know how things will turn out. All you have is the "spectacular" now.

Arkopaul

I always believe in expecting the worst. No, it doesn't make me more anxious, I am anxious anyway. When I expect the worst, and it happens, I don't get disappointed, and if something better happens it makes me feel better. But if I expect the best and the best doesn't happen, I will be disappointed. Expecting the worst clearly has its perks.

Arkopaul

It sucks when you had so many reasons to give up on them but you chose to ignore it all and stay, but they you left anyway.

Some people will become strangers with all your secrets and you simply have to live with that thought because there is nothing you can do to change it.

Arkopaul

Some people are perfect in every way but that doesn't mean they are for you. That doesn't mean they will know how to treat you right or vibe along to the things you enjoy. Then there will be some people who are super imperfect but somehow you will hit it off with them brilliantly, because they are made for you.

Arkopaul

There are some people who will break your heart but fix your vision.

Arkopaul

We tolerate so much pain and bullshit because we feel like this is what we deserve, that we can't get any better than this. We settle for less.

Arkopaul

"It is what it is" is not a solution. It is a trauma response.

Arkopaul

Most people who grew up getting bullied and abused are billionaires right now. Don't let the past show who you are supposed to be. Ignore everyone until you reach the top because when you do, they will come to you.

Arkopaul

You cannot recover yesterday.

Arkopaul

Hope is beautiful and dangerous at the same time. Hope is what kills us and also builds us. Hope is what keeps us going and also breaks up apart every time. Hope keeps us alive and kills us every day. Hope is ironic and meaningful, but if we don't have hope, what do we even have?

Arkopaul

You need to face and conquer your fears.

Arkopaul

Everything I was afraid to lose, I lost.

Arkopaul

You can cry and beg and procrastinate all you want but time isn't stopping for you. It will go on with or without you. Better hop on the time train and go along with it instead of getting left behind.

Arkopaul

You will stop living for other people and caring about what they feel about you once you realise how soon they forget the dead. Death is the most severe and permanent outcome of life, and people still forget and move on with their own lives. So why live your life for them?

Arkopaul

There's a popular saying that "If he could do it, why can't you?" or "There's nothing you can't do." But this is not true. Not everyone is built the same way. It doesn't matter how much hard work and practice you put in, there's always something you won't be able to do because your body, mind, and just your life is built differently. Stephen Hawking can't win a race against Usain Bolt and similarly Usain Bolt probably couldn't have discovered black holes. To each its own, so find your niche and stick to it.

Arkopaul

Slow down if needed but don't stop.

Arkopaul

I don't know who needs to hear this, but You were not wrong; you did everything you could. Your heart was pure and you loved them, simply. You were never the problem, they were. You are precious and anyone would be lucky to have you in their life.

Arkopaul

You were not the only flower in his garden.

Arkopaul

Sometimes the love that brings you together fails to overwhelm the pain that tears you apart.

Arkopaul

This is something Paulo Coelho once said "Tears are words that need to be written" and I couldn't agree more.

Arkopaul

The world won't ever stop for you to grief. It won't care. It will go on with or without you. So better wipe your tears and get back up on your feet as fast you can.

Arkopaul

People who love you won't quit on you. What is meant for you, will.

Arkopaul

People underestimate the peace of sitting in your room, eating your favourite food, watching your favourite Tv show while cuddling with your dog.

Arkopaul

At some point you will stop on your path, turn around and tell yourself "This ain't what I wanna keep going through, this ain't what I deserve." and you will leave.

Arkopaul

The only person you should compare yourself is to the person you were yesterday. In fact, fuck that, don't even compare yourself to your past self. You are not that dumbfuck anymore.

Arkopaul

My life has been fucked up and I have done some good and bad things but I don't regret a single thing that I did or that happened to me. I can't change whatever happened and deep inside I know I am a good fucking person so if I did someone wrong, they probably deserved that shit.

Arkopaul

The urge to flex after you went through a break up is strong. I get it. You want to show off that you are great, it didn't affect you, you are going to the club, to the gym, to parties, you are meeting new people and shit, but at the end of the day you are doing all these just to flex and fill that void in your heart. You will soon grow tired and drained and you will not have moved on. You are simply holding on to them by flexing to them. It's not worth it, let it go.

Arkopaul

Commitment isn't scary but wasting another couple of years of my life, is.

Arkopaul

I don't know who said this but this one thing never leaves my mind. "If you can't make money while you sleep, you have to work till you die." This is my daily mantra and I want to get to a point in my life where I don't have to work or worry about money anymore. Where I can simply, be.

Arkopaul

Behind every successful and strong person is a story that gave them no choice.

Arkopaul

Do a bit of meditation and yoga even if you find it bullshit. If you could flirt around and ruin months of your life over someone who didn't give a shit about you, you can probably waste like 20 mins everyday meditating or doing yoga. Do it.

Arkopaul

I don't hate anyone in this world. If you did something to me that would make me hate you then trust me, I don't even remember who you are anymore, you don't exist to me. I have made my peace with the pain I received from you and I simply don't care anymore.

Arkopaul

Sometimes you have to be quiet even when you are exploding with feelings and have a lot to say. There's no point oversharing to people who caused you to feel this way in the first place.

Arkopaul

I never had friends and I don't know a lot about friendships but one thing I am sure of is that you never betray or backstab or back bitch about each other.

Arkopaul

All relationships are a risk, things might not turn out the way you had imagined and it's okay. Don't be afraid to give your heart as long as it's healed already.

Arkopaul

Love is basically handing someone a loaded gun and expecting them to not shoot you.

Arkopaul

They will swear that they don't want to lose you and yet they will consistently act like they don't want to keep you. What's up with that?

Arkopaul

Someone is probably mad, talking shit about you right now just because you chose distance over drama and disrespect.

Once you shift your focus and start working on yourself and become confident, you will start attracting the kind of people you actually want to be with.

Arkopaul

There are people waking up, smiling and going to work every morning while fighting a thousand demons in their head every night. We really have become a pro at hiding shit, haven't we?

Arkopaul

If they come back, don't forget how broken you were when they left.

Arkopaul

I never had any idol or any inspiration because I always believed in myself and wanted to be my own inspiration. I know all the shit I have been through; I truly know what my heart wants and how pure it is, there is literally no one purer than me.

Arkopaul

There isn't any closure. Stop looking for it and move the fuck on.

Arkopaul

I am done trying to look cool to impress other people. From now on, I will be hot.

Arkopaul

I have this amazing ability to bounce back from literally whatever life throws at me. Every time I fell down, I got back right up. If I didn't, I wouldn't be here writing this shit today. But I do get tired, I am only human.

Arkopaul

The society won't pay your bills or put food on your plate. Stop living for them and start living for yourself.

Arkopaul

I don't just wanna be rich, I wanna be unreachable.

Arkopaul

You have lived in the darkness and let people walk over you for so long that you can't see the light that you radiate and just how fucking beautiful you truly are.

Arkopaul

It's okay to not feel okay all the time. We are only human and we are supposed to feel a variety of emotions. We are supposed to be in touch with all our sides, the happy and the depressed ones. But never let someone else dictate how you are supposed to feel.

Arkopaul

Overthinking is sort of a super power because you have already seen all 14 million possibilities and solutions before approaching any problem.

Arkopaul

Never be embarrassed about having less money than others, having old parents, having responsibilities to take care of. You are the doing the best you can and you are probably more talented than all the other people who aren't doing jack.

Arkopaul

Do you ever feel like you are handling the situations a lot better than your old self would have? You are standing tall and strong and weathering all the storms while if your old self was faced with these circumstances, he probably would have been super broken up about it.

Arkopaul

Lastly, I would urge everyone to not force anything. Not relationships, not jobs, not your studies, career, family, basically don't force anything in your life. Let this shit flow and go along with it, be happy, have fun, be depressed as well when you need to be and above all be a bad bitch and kick some asses.

Arkopaul

"I have bad posture because I hate myself."

- Pete Davidson.

Arkopaul Das is a self-published writer, streamer, youtuber, poet, blogger, trader and a self-proclaimed cinephile. He loves all things aesthetic and considers himself to have a creative mind. His other books consist of the infamous "Insomniac" and "Sociopath: Deceitful Game".

Arkopaul

Arkopaul

www.ingramcontent.com/pod-product-compliance
Lightning Source LLC
Chambersburg PA
CBHW071320140726
47996CB00005B/1743